Mandala
STAINED GLASS
PATTERN BOOK
Anna Croyle

DOVER PUBLICATIONS, INC.
MINEOLA, NEW YORK

Copyright

Bibliographical Note

Mandala Stained Glass Pattern Book is a new work, first published by Dover Publications, Inc., in 2008.

DOVER *Pictorial Archive* SERIES

International Standard Book Number

ISBN-13: 978-0-486-46605-7
ISBN-10: 0-486-46605-1

Manufactured in the United States by Courier Corporation
46605102
www.doverpublications.com

Note

Mandala is from the Sanskrit word for circle. These complex circular designs are used in Hindu, Christian, and Native American healing rituals and meditation traditions. By drawing the eye inward to the center, these layered symmetrical designs encourage concentration, thereby promoting a meditative state.

Beyond their meditative powers, mandalas are simply beautiful to look at. They feature shapes, patterns, and creatures from the natural world. Crescents, crosses, spirals, stars, fish, flowers, branches, and vines are just a few of the mandala designs you will find within.

Inside are ninety-nine patterns you can reproduce in smaller or larger sizes. They are readily adaptable for use in windows, mirrors, mobiles, ornaments, lampshades, and other craft applications. All materials needed, including general instructions and tools for beginners, can be purchased from local craft and hobby stores, or on the Internet.

1

3

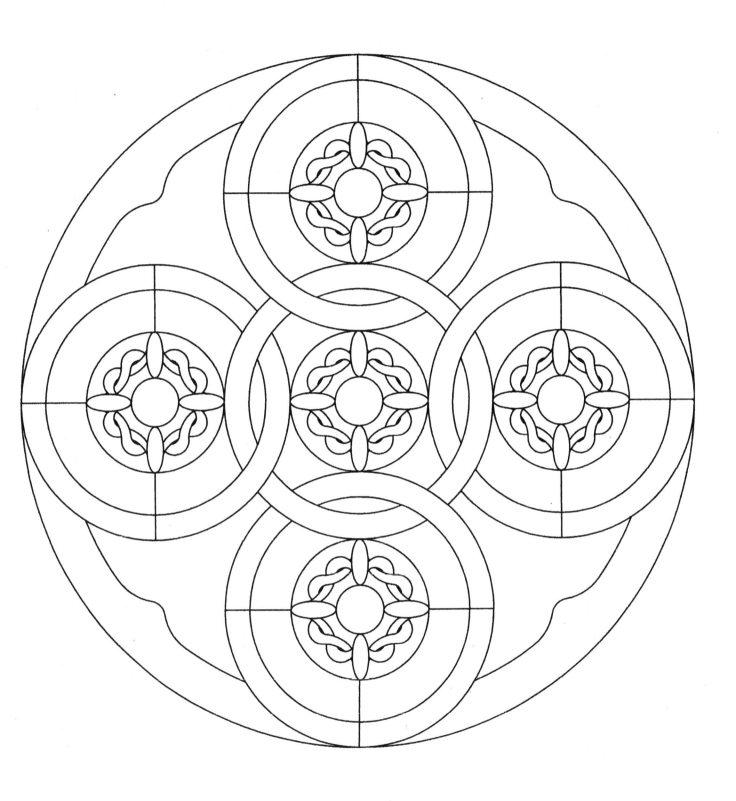

8

9

14

15

24

34

41

43

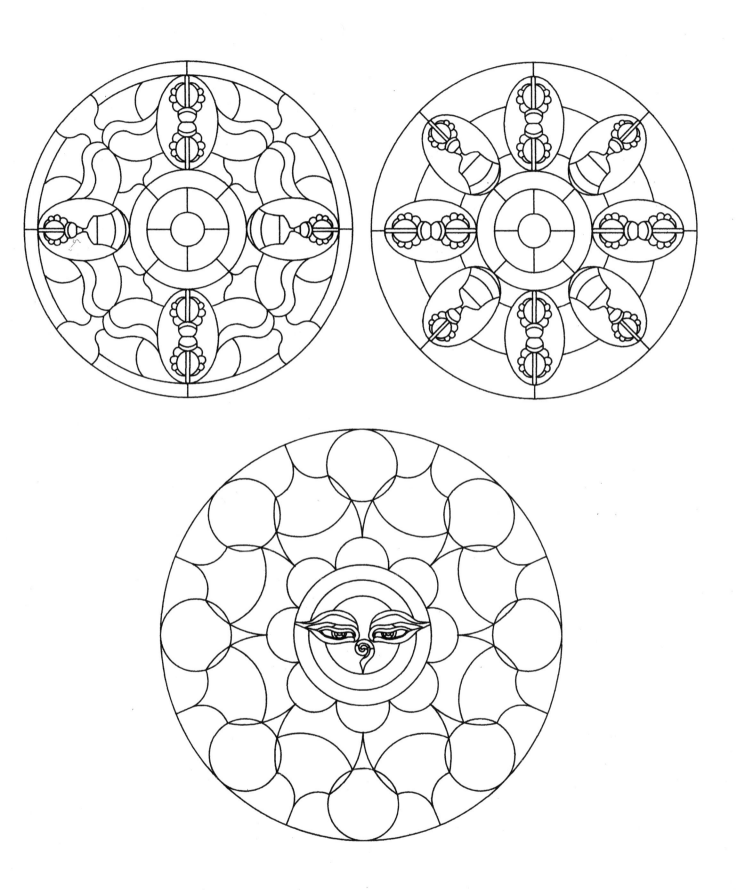

47

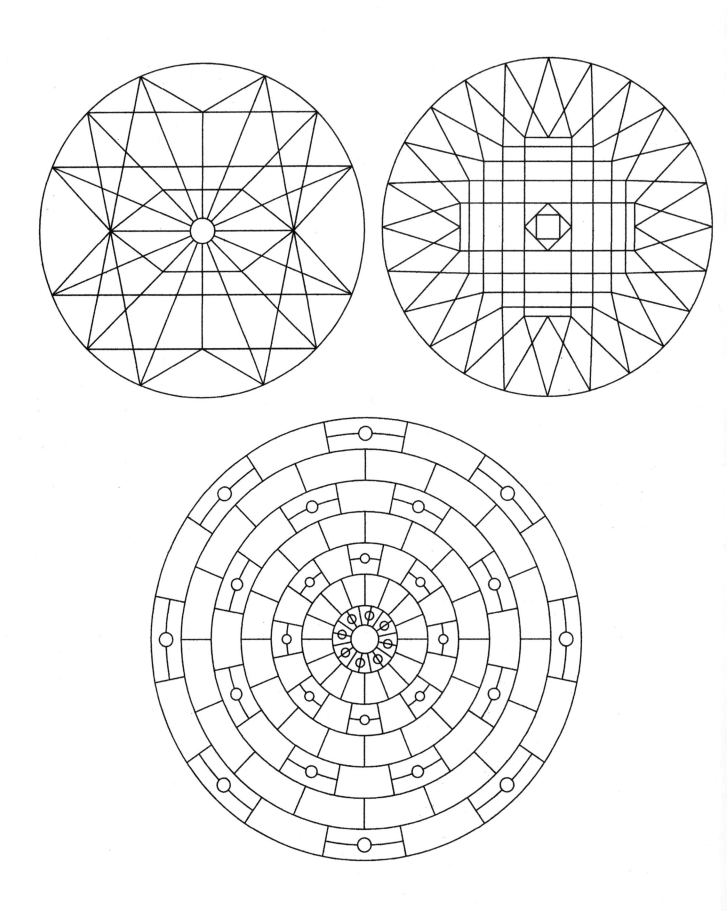

49

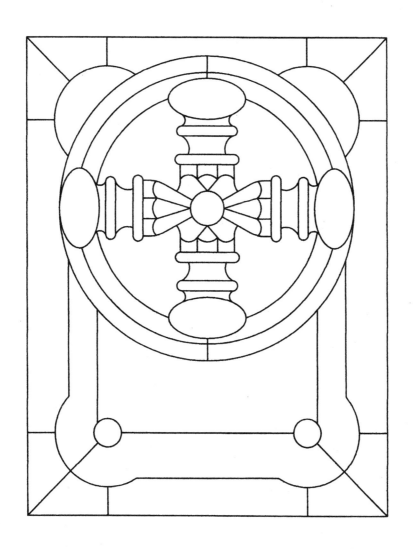

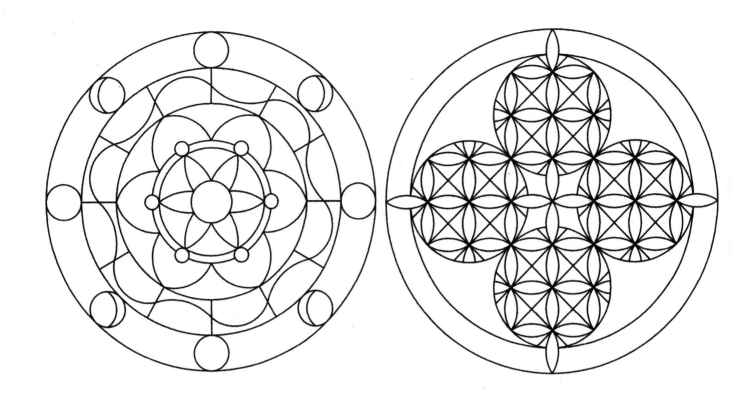